2002

Robin—

Happy
Chanukah!
I saw this and
thought you would
enjoy it — You've even have
some wisdom of
your own to add
to it. I Love You—
Deb

THE WISDOM OF
JUDAISM

Compiled by Victor Malka
Paintings by Marc Chagall

Abbeville Press   Publishers
New York   London   Paris

Cover illustration and vignettes by Danielle Siegelbaum

For the English-language edition
RESEARCH, TRANSLATION FROM THE FRENCH, AND BIBLIOGRAPHY:
John O'Toole
EDITOR: Jacqueline Decter
TYPOGRAPHIC DESIGN: Virginia Pope
PRODUCTION EDITOR: Owen Dugan

For the original edition
SERIES EDITORS: Marc de Smedt and Michel Piquemal
DESIGNER: Dominique Guillaumin/Cédric Ramadier

First edition
10 9 8 7 6 5 4 3 2 1

Library of Congress Cataloging-in-Publication Data

Paroles de sagesse juive. English.
The wisdom of Judaism/compiled by Victor Malka; paintings by
Marc Chagall.
p. cm.
Includes bibliographical references.
ISBN 0-7892-0236-0
1. Judaism—Quotations, maxims, etc. I. Malka, Victor. II.
Chagall, Marc, 1887–   . III. Title.
BM43.P37 1996
296—dc20   96–16439

Rather than builders of empires or cathedrals, throughout the several thousand years of their history the Jews have been more like "builders of time," as one of their thinkers, Abraham Heschel, put it, because they set up "palaces" in time, namely, the Sabbath and the holidays. They have devoted the greatest share of their energy, however, to investigating the world and seeking to acquire wisdom. Along with patience, wisdom is, as Friedrich Dürrenmatt affirmed, one of the "two sole gifts that history has given Israel."

This wisdom, which Jews have always made at one and the same time a preoccupation, an ideal, and an objective, aims to bring out the best within each individual. Judaism considers wisdom to be a major quality, to such an extent that King Solomon—whom the Jewish tradition calls "the wisest of men" and to whom is attributed the authorship of the Biblical Book of Proverbs—wrote, "Say unto wisdom, Thou art my sister; and call understanding thy kinsman" (Proverbs 7:4).

In thousands of texts the Jewish tradition emphasizes the need above all to acquire wisdom. This is indeed one of the great enduring themes of a tradition that runs from the Old Testament to the great Jewish writers of the twentieth century and includes the principal schools of Jewish thought, such as medieval Jewish philosophy, the Cabbala, and Hasidism.

What does this wisdom tell us? It says first of all that man is free to become whatever he wishes, for if he were not a free moral agent, nothing would have real meaning. He must never lose sight of the fact that genuine faith in one God is measured by the love we feel for others. He must remember that life is a gift granted to us by God, and that if we put our mind to it the world can shine with joy.

Wisdom, in the lyrical expression that the Jewish tradition has given it, also says that we must learn never to lose our footing, as it were, to reject solitude and egoism—which are at times one and the same thing. Wisdom is to know that within all men lies the possibility of redeeming themselves, that nothing is ever lost, and that self-control is needed in all aspects of life. It teaches us to recall as well that, as the greatest Jewish philosopher Moses Maimonides put it, "The straight path is the most exact middle course through man's inclinations: courage lies between temerity and cowardice; dignity, between haughtiness and vulgarity; humility, between arrogance and servility; modesty, between impudence and timidity." Finally, wisdom tells us to bear in mind that any exile can be transformed into something spiritual.

Subtly interwoven throughout the texts of the Bible, all of the above was to be reaffirmed and underscored in the early years of the Christian era by the masters of the Talmud, a compilation of ancient teachings consisting of the Mishnah (collection of originally oral laws) and the Gemara (commentaries on and elaborations of the Mishnah). Yet it was in the literature that began to develop in the eighteenth century around the masters of the popular religious movement known as Hasidism—whose foremost leaders included the movement's founder, Baal Shem Tov, along with Nahman of Bratslav and Dov Baer of Mezritch—that this wisdom would find its most elegant voice, its most universal aesthetic, and its most authentic spokesmen.

Hasidism stressed the obligation to love "even the wicked," the need to avoid being exiled from ourselves and, when our soul is troubled, to ask ourselves first, "What is it that I want?" As these masters say over and over in thousands of aphorisms that have since passed into legend, we must renew ourselves each day. At the same time, we musn't think only of ourselves for we then become "idolaters." We must always temper our anger with compassion, they add, and seek peace with the help of the truth, because where there is no truth, "there is neither grace nor faith."

Like their predecessors of the Talmud and the Cabbala, these masters teach detachment from the self, what they call *bittul ha-yesh* ("annihilation of selfhood"), the quest for both a rigorous ethics for leading our lives and a humanism with a universal aim. From the words of the Talmud's Tractate Avoth, and later the Hasidic movement's own contribution, right up to the writings of Martin Buber in our century, a continuity and a number of common denominators run throughout this tradition. The words of these figures, brought together here, bear witness to one and the same source. It is a wisdom that lives still.

Victor Malka

Man should always have two pockets.

In one he shall write,

"I am but dust and ashes."

In the other,

"The world was created for me alone."

Bunem of Przysucha

Noah and the Rainbow

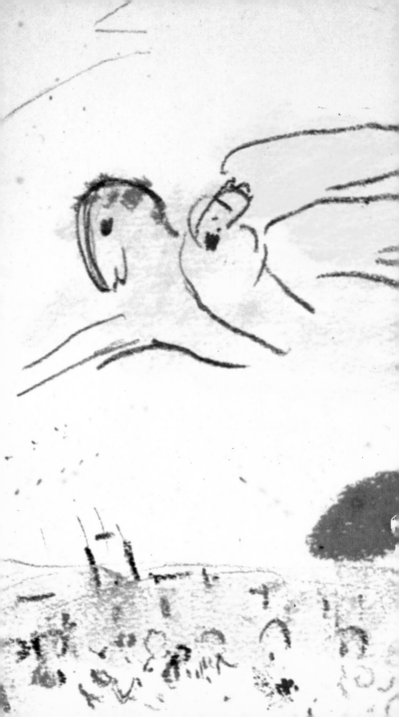

Just as a hand held before your eyes hides the highest mountain, so our petty day-to-day life hinders us from seeing the fantastic lights and secrets that fill the world. He who is able to put life from his eyes shall see the intense brilliance of the inner world.

Nahman of Bratslav

Ben Zoma said,
"Who is wise?
   He that learns from all men....
Who is mighty?
   One who subdues his passions....
Who is rich?
   He who rejoiceth in his portion....
Who is honored?
   One that honors his fellow men."

Talmud, *Tractate Avoth* (4.1)

Moses and Aaron (detail)

Temptation is but a trial:

it is then that you must reveal

what is pure metal in you.

Isaac Meir of Ger

When thou cuttest down thine harvest in thy field, and hast forgot a sheaf in the field, thou shalt not go again to fetch it: it shall be for the stranger, for the fatherless, and for the widow, that the Lord thy God may bless thee in all the work of thine hands.

When thou beatest thine olive tree, thou shalt not go over the boughs again: it shall be for the stranger, for the fatherless, and for the widow.

When thou gatherest the grapes of thy vineyard, thou shalt not glean it afterward: it shall be for the stranger, for the fatherless, and for the widow.

And thou shalt remember that thou wast a bondman in the land of Egypt: therefore I command thee to do this thing.

Deuteronomy 24:19–22

Jacob Leaves His Homeland to Go down into Egypt (detail)

Free will is offered to all men. If they wish to follow the path of goodness and become righteous, the will to do so is in their hands, and if they wish to follow the path of evil and become wicked, the will to do so is also in their hands.

Maimonides

The Creation of Man (detail)

When you fathom the life of things and of conditionality,

you reach the indissoluble;

when you dispute the life of things and of conditionality,

you wind up before the nothing;

when you consecrate life,

you encounter the living God.

Martin Buber (1878–1965)

The Song of Songs V

We must live in joy.

We must live in love.

They are moreover one and the same thing.

Moses of Kobrin

Every day we must dance, if only in our thoughts.

Nahman of Bratslav

The Emperor said to Rabbi Joshua ben Hananiah, "I wish to see your God."

He replied, "You cannot see him."

"Indeed," said the Emperor, "I will see him."

He went and placed the Emperor facing the sun during the summer solstice and said to him, "Look up at it."

He replied, "I cannot."

Said Rabbi Joshua, "If at the sun which is but one of the ministers that attend the Holy One, blessed be He, you cannot look, how then can you presume to look upon the divine presence!"

Talmud, *Tractate Hullin* 59b–60a

Study for Moses before the Burning Bush (detail)

One day Rabbi Elimelekh of Lizhensk sent his disciples on the eve of Yom Kippur, the Day of Atonement, to observe the behavior of a tailor. "You shall learn from him," said he, "what a man must do on this holy day." Through a window they saw the tailor take down from the shelf a book in which he had noted all the sins he had committed over the entire year. With his book in hand the tailor addressed God thus:

"Today is the day of atonement for all the people of Israel; the time has come for both of us, You, my God, and I, to settle our accounts. Here is the list of all my sins, but here is another where I have noted down all the transgressions You have committed, the worries, the sadness, and the sorrow You have caused me and my family. Master of the World, if we tallied up the total exactly, You would owe me far me than I owe You. But today is Yom Kippur, when it is each man's duty to make peace with his neighbor. So I shall forgive You Your transgressions if You forgive me mine. Master of the World, let peace and joy reign between us."

Shmuel Yosef Agnon, *Yamim noraim (The Days of Awe)*

It happened that a certain heathen came before Shammai and said to him, "Make me a proselyte, on condition that you teach me the whole Torah while I stand on one foot." Thereupon he repulsed him with the builder's cubit which was in his hand.

When he went before Hillel, he said to him, "What is hateful to you, do not to your neighbor: that is the whole Torah, while the rest is the commentary thereof; go and learn it."

Talmud, *Tractate Shabbath* 31a

Moses and Aaron before Pharaoh (detail)

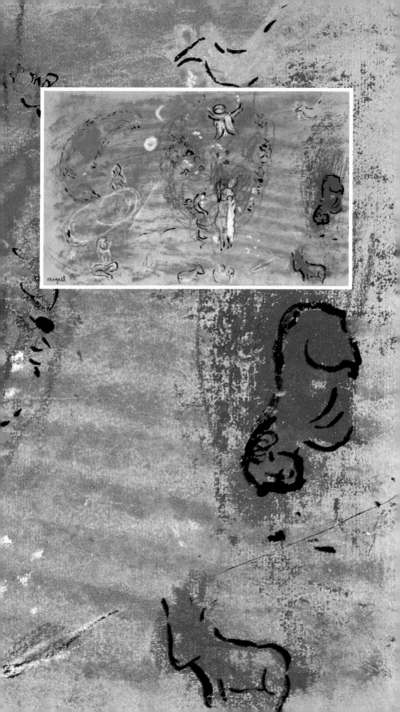

Thus was the world created:

all men must know how to give and to receive.

He who does not know how to do one as much

as the other resembles a barren tree.

Isaac Eizik of Zhidachov

Seven are an abomination unto him:

A proud look,
a lying tongue,
and hands that shed innocent blood,
an heart that deviseth wicked imaginations,
feet that be swift in running to mischief,
a false witness that speaketh lies,
and he that soweth discord among brethren.

Proverbs 6:16–19

Cain and Abel

A favorite saying of the Rabbis of Jabneh was:

I am God's creature and my fellow is God's creature.
My work is in the town and his work is in the coun-
try. I rise early for my work and he rises early for his
work. Just as he does not presume to do my work, so I

Jacob's Dream

do not presume to do his work. Will you say, "I do much and he does little"? We have learnt: One may do much or one may do little; it is all one, provided he directs his heart to heaven.

Talmud, *Tractate Berakoth* 17a

From him who seeks greatness, greatness flees,

but him who flees greatness, greatness follows.

Talmud, *Tractate Erubin* 13b

Why was man created on the last day?

So that if he is overcome by pride it might be said:

"In the creation of the world,

the mosquito came before you."

Midrash Rabba, Genesis

Despise not any man, and discard not any thing,

for there is not a man who has not his hour and

there exists not a thing which has not its place.

Talmud, *Tractate Avoth* 4.3

If I am not for myself, who will be for me....

And if not now, when?

Talmud, *Tractate Avoth* 1.14

Study for The Song of Songs II

Rabbi Eleazar also said:

Fasting is more efficacious than charity. What is the reason? One is performed with a man's money, the other with his body.

Talmud, *Tractate Berakoth* 32b

Abraham and the Three Angels (detail)

When man comes into the world his hands are closed as if to say, "The whole world is mine, I want to possess it."

When he leaves the world his hands are spread wide as if to say, "I possessed nothing of what is in the present world."

Midrash Rabba, Ecclesiastes

From the child you can learn three things:

He is merry for no particular reason;

Never for a moment is he idle;

When he needs something, he demands it vigorously.

Dov Baer of Mezritch

Study for The Song of Songs II (detail)

He told me:
My race is yellow.
I answered:
I'm of your race.

He told me:
My race is black.
I answered:
I'm of your race.

He told me:
My race is white.
I answered:
I'm of your race

for my sun was the yellow star,
for I am wrapped in night,
for my soul, like the tables of the law,
is white.

Edmond Jabès, *Art contre/against Apartheid*

Study for Abraham and the Three Angels

Marc Chagall
(1887-1985)

Born in Russia, the painter, draftsman, engraver, and sculptor Marc Chagall came from a highly religious Jewish family.

All of the paintings illustrating the texts in this volume come from the Musée National "Message Biblique" Marc Chagall in Nice. Chagall's daily reading of the Bible, "the greatest source of poetry for all time," as the artist himself put it, inspired these pictures.

In 1973 the artist donated this exceptional collection to France, with the fond hope that it would be housed along the shores of the Mediterranean as a way of "giving back to a region [he] loved its share of light."

"In my mind these paintings do not represent the dream of a single people, but that of humanity."

Selected Bibliography

General approaches to Judaism and Jewish culture throughout the ages:

Alter, Robert. *The Art of Biblical Narrative*. New York: Basic Books, 1981. (Professor of Hebrew and comparative literature, Mr. Alter offers a literary critic's approach to the Old Testament.)

Armstrong, Karen. *A History of God: The 4,000-Year Quest of Judaism, Christianity, and Islam*. New York: Ballantine, 1993.

Ausubel, Nathan, ed. *A Treasury of Jewish Folklore: Stories, Traditions, Legends, Humor, Wisdom, and Folksongs of the Jewish People*. New York: Crown, 1948 (reprint 1975).

Ben Shea, Noah. *The Word: An Anthology of Jewish Wisdom Through Time*. New York: Villard, 1995.

Blenkinsopp, Joseph. *The Pentateuch: An Introduction to the First Five Books of the Bible*. New York: Doubleday, 1992.

Cahn-Lipman, Rabbi David E. *The Book of Jewish Knowledge: 613 Basic Facts about Judaism*. Northvale, N.J.: Jason Aronson, 1991.

Greenberg, Rabbi Irving. *The Jewish Way: A Comprehensive and Inspiring Presentation of Judaism as Revealed Through Its Holy Days*. New York: Simon and Schuster, 1988.

Gross, David C., and Esther R. Gross. *Jewish Wisdom: A Treasury of Proverbs, Maxims, Aphorisms, Wise Sayings, and Memorable Quotations*. New York: Fawcett Crest, 1992.

On the Talmud, the Cabbala, Jewish mysticism, and Hasidism:

Ariel, David S. *The Mystic Quest: An Introduction to Jewish Mysticism*. New York: Schocken, 1989.

Bader, Gershom. *The Encyclopedia of Talmudic Sages*. Northvale, N.J.: Jason Aronson, 1988.

Ben-Amos, Dan, and Jerome R. Mintz, trs. and eds. *In Praise of the Baal Shem Tov: The Earliest Collection of Legends About the Founder of Hasidism*. Northvale, N.J.: Jason Aronson, 1993.

Cohen, Abraham. *Everyman's Talmud: The Major Teachings of the Rabbinic Sages*. New York: Schocken, 1949 (reprint 1995).

Dan, Joseph, ed. *The Teachings of Hasidism*. West Orange, N.J.: Behrman House, 1983.

Eliach, Yaffa, *Hasidic Tales of the Holocaust*. New York: Vintage, 1988.

Sarna, Nahum M., general ed. *The Torah Commentary*. Philadelphia, New York, Jerusalem: Jewish Publication Society, 1989. (A new English translation and commentary of the Talmud in a handsome, bilingual edition.)

Steinsaltz, Rabbi Adin. *The Talmud: The Steinsaltz Edition, a Reference Guide*. New York: Random House, 1989. (An illustrated guide through the intricate paths of Talmudic logic and thought.)

A collection of the writings of Moses Maimonides, the greatest medieval Jewish philosopher, has been brought out by Dover in their Philosophy and Religion series: *Ethical Writings of Maimonides*. New York: Dover, 1983. See also *The Epistles of Maimonides: Crisis and Leadership*. Halkin, Abraham, tr. and notes. Philadelphia, Jerusalem: The Jewish Publication Society, 1993 (paper).

Finally, the above list would be sorely lacking if we failed to mention Leo Rosten's *The Joys of Yiddish*, a "relaxed lexicon of Yiddish, Hebrew and Yinglish words" spiritedly illustrated with "serendipitous excursions" into Jewish folklore, customs, cuisine, tales, and, jokes.